THIS BOOK BELONGS TO:

_____

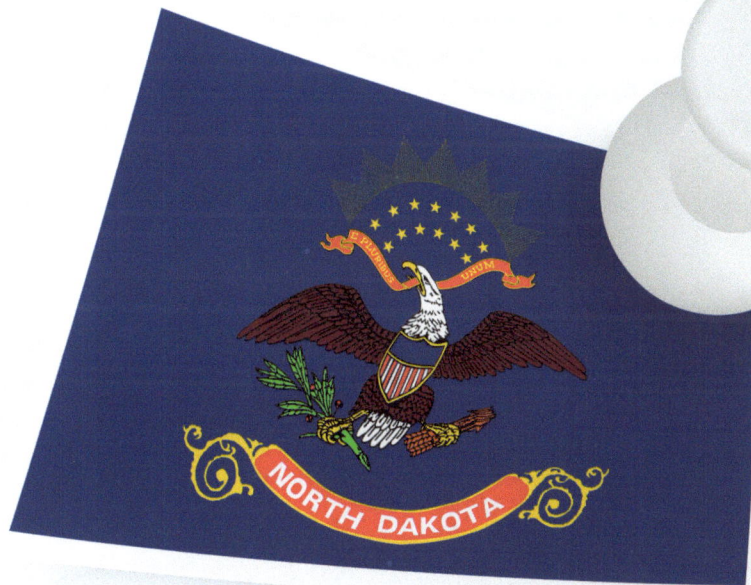

WELCOME
TO
NORTH DACOTA

Dedicated to all the explorers.

ISBN 978-1-958985-81-6

www.joeysavestheday.com

A Mimi Book

North Dakota got its name from the Dakota Sioux people. The word "Dakota" means "friend" or "ally" in their language. When the Dakota Territory was split in 1889, the northern part became North Dakota, keeping the name to honor the Native heritage of the land.

North Dakota was the thirty-ninth state to join the Union. It officially joined on November 2, 1889.

39th

North Dakota is located in the upper Midwestern region of the United States and is bordered by three states: Minnesota, South Dakota, and Montana.

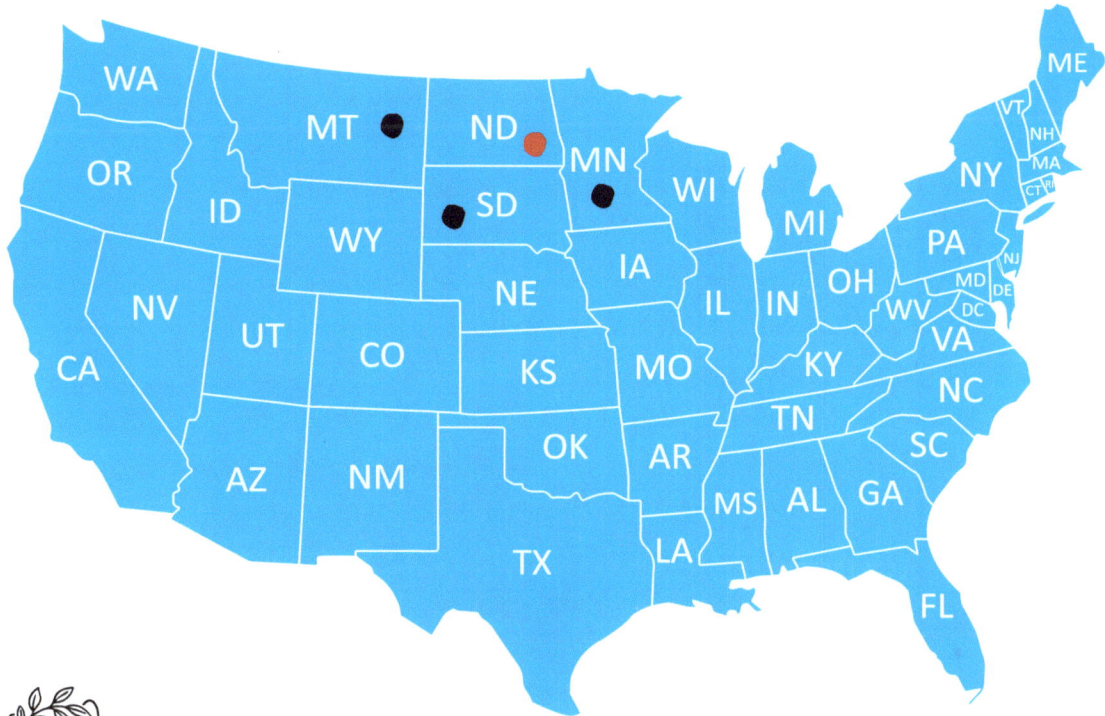

Bismarck is the capital of North Dakota.
It officially became the capital in 1889.

Bismarck, North Dakota, has an estimated population of about 77,770 people.

Railroad Bridge over the Missouri River in Bismarck , North Dakota.

North Dakota ranks as the nineteenth largest state in the United States in terms of area.

North Dakota

The Badlands in North Dakota.

There are approximately 796,560 people residing in North Dakota.

Grand Forks, North Dakota

David Henderson Houston (1841–1906) was a Scottish-born farmer in North Dakota who changed photography forever. Living near Hunter, he invented roll film and patented a small, portable camera in 1881. His ideas made cameras lighter, cheaper, and easier to use. Houston later sold his patents to George Eastman, whose Kodak cameras brought photography into everyday homes.

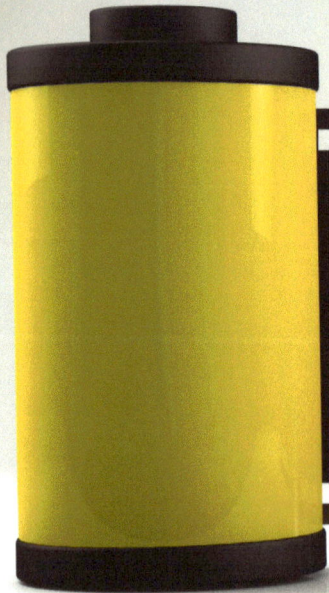

Juneberry pie crumb cake is one of the most beloved foods in North Dakota. Juneberries grow wild across the prairie, and they taste a little like a mix of blueberries and almonds. Families pick them in the summer and freeze them so they can bake pies all year long.

North Dakota

There are 53 counties in North Dakota.

Here is a list of twenty of those counties:

Benson	Foster	Mercer	Stutsman
Bottineau	Grant	Oliver	Towner
Burleigh	Kidder	Renville	Walsh
Cavalier	McHenry	Sargent	Ward
Divide	McKenzie	Sioux	Williams

Devils Lake is the largest natural lake in North Dakota and is known for its constantly changing water levels. The lake sits in a closed basin, which means water can only leave by evaporation or when the lake gets high enough to spill into nearby waterways. Over the years, Devils Lake has grown and shrunk many times, creating new shorelines and shaping the surrounding landscape.

NATURAL

The International Peace Garden sits directly on the border between the North Dakota and Canada and was created in 1932 to honor the peaceful relationship between the two nations. The garden covers more than 2,300 acres of flowers, lakes, and forests, and visitors can even stand with one foot in each country. It remains one of the world's largest symbols of international friendship and cooperation.

The Liberty Memorial Bridge was the first big car bridge to connect Bismarck and Mandan across the Missouri River. It opened in 1922 and was built to honor North Dakota's World War I veterans. For many years, it helped people travel safely between the two cities and became an important part of daily life. A new bridge replaced the old one in 2008, but it still carries the same name and the same sense of history.

North Dakota's Badlands are a rugged, colorful landscape filled with striped hills, deep canyons, and strange rock shapes carved by wind and water. Even though the name sounds harsh, the area is full of quiet beauty and wildlife like bison, wild horses, and prairie dogs. These Badlands are mostly found inside Theodore Roosevelt National Park, which protects some of the most dramatic scenery in the state.

The North Dakota state bird is
the Western Meadowlark. It was
chosen as the state bird in 1947.

NORTH
DAKOTA

The official state flower of North Dakota is the Wild Prairie Rose. It was chosen as the state flower on March 7, 1907.

Wild

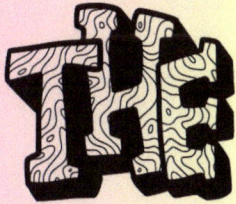   

~ And ~

The North Dakota state motto, "Liberty and Union, Now and Forever, One and Inseparable," was officially adopted in 1889.

 AND

NOW! And FOREVER

 And

NORTH DAKOTA
NORTH DAKOTA
NORTH DAKOTA
NORTH DAKOTA

The abbreviation for North Dakota is ND.

ND

North Dakota's state flag was officially adopted in 1911.

Some crops grown in North Dakota are barley, black beans, lentils, and soybeans.

Some animals that live in North Dakota are black bears, bighorn sheep, bison, coyotes, moose, and squirrels.

North Dakota experiences extreme temperatures that vary significantly throughout the year. The highest recorded temperature in the state was 121 degrees Fahrenheit, reached in Steele on July 6, 1936. Conversely, the coldest temperature recorded was -60 degrees Fahrenheit (60 degrees below zero) in Parshall on February 15, 1936.

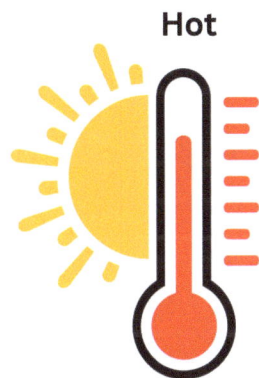

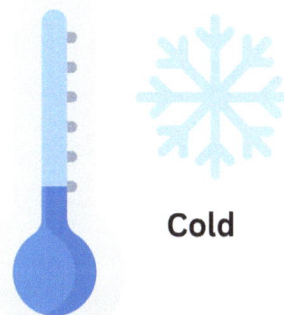

Hot

Cold

ZOO

The Dakota Zoo sits right along the Missouri River in Bismarck, and it's the biggest zoo in the state. Kids can meet all kinds of animals here, from tigers and penguins to camels, monkeys, and bright tropical birds.

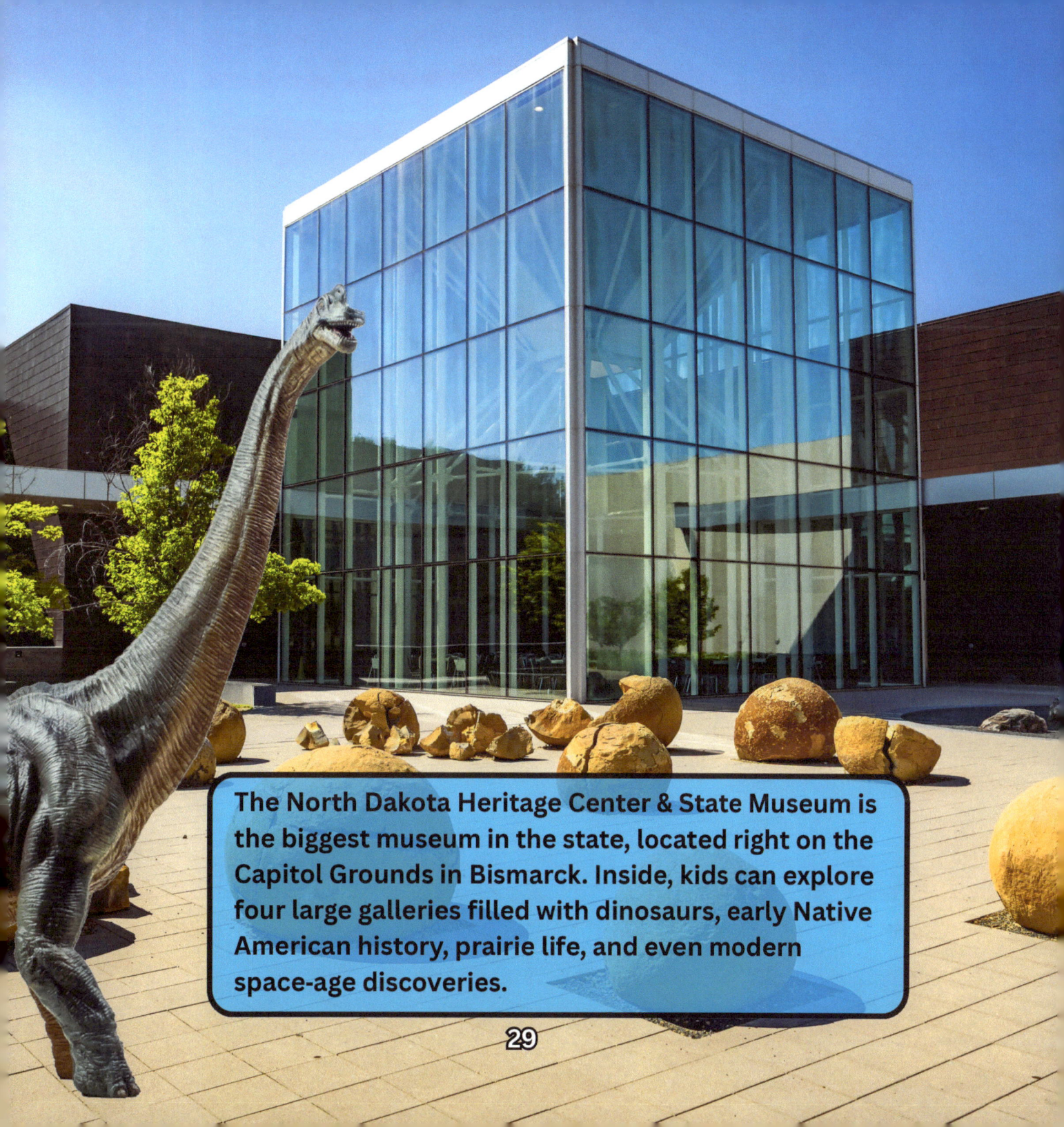

The North Dakota Heritage Center & State Museum is the biggest museum in the state, located right on the Capitol Grounds in Bismarck. Inside, kids can explore four large galleries filled with dinosaurs, early Native American history, prairie life, and even modern space-age discoveries.

Hector International Airport is the busiest airport in North Dakota, and it's located in Fargo, on the eastern side of the state near the Minnesota border. You can find it at 2801 32nd Avenue North, Fargo, North Dakota. Even though it's called "international," most of its flights travel to cities across the United States, like Denver, Chicago, and Phoenix.

The Fargo-Moorhead RedHawks are North Dakota's most well-known baseball team. They play in Fargo, on the eastern side of the state, at Newman Outdoor Field, a bright and family-friendly ballpark. The RedHawks are part of the American Association of Professional Baseball, an independent league where talented players compete at a high level.

FOOTBALL

The North Dakota State Bison are the most famous football team in the state, and they play in Fargo, on the eastern side of North Dakota. Their home field is the Fargodome, an indoor stadium that gets incredibly loud when fans cheer for the Bison. The team is known for its winning tradition and has earned many national championships in college football's FCS division.

The American Elm is North Dakota's state tree. It grows tall and strong, with branches that spread out like a giant umbrella. This hardy tree can survive freezing winters and has been a familiar sight across the state for generations. Even though a disease called Dutch elm disease has harmed many elms, the trees that stay healthy can live for hundreds of years.

The Northern Pike is North Dakota's state fish. It's a long, fast swimmer with a mouth full of tiny sharp teeth and spots along its green body. Northern pike love hiding in weedy lakes and rivers, where they wait quietly before zooming out to catch their food.

Can you name these?

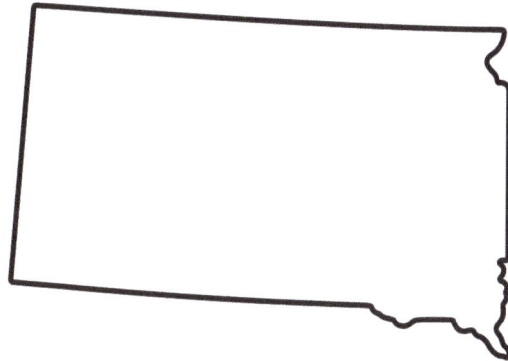

I hope you enjoyed
learning about
North Dakota.

To explore fun facts about the other 49 states,
visit my website at www.joeysavestheday.com.
You'll also find a wide variety of homeschool
resources to support joyful learning at home.
If you enjoyed this book, I would be grateful if
you left a review. Your feedback truly helps.
Thank you for your support!

TIME
TO SAY
GOODBYE

Check out these other interesting books in the 50 States Fact Books Series!

OHIO FACTS

Pennsylvania FACTS

TEXAS FACTS

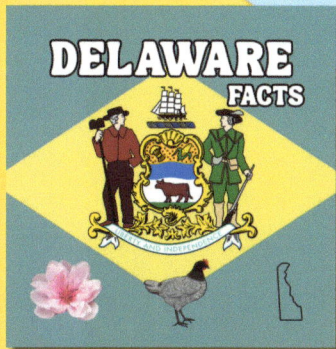

DELAWARE FACTS

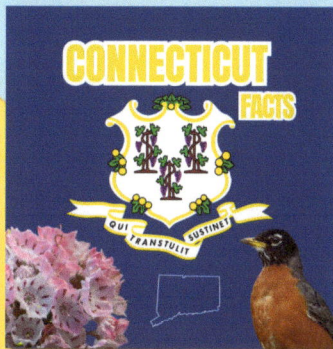

CONNECTICUT FACTS

KENTUCKY FACTS

GEORGIA FACTS

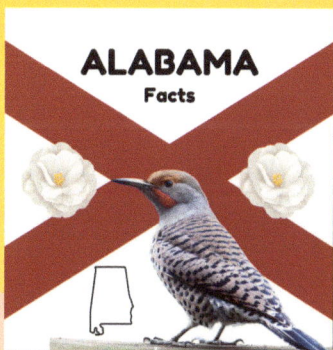

ALABAMA Facts

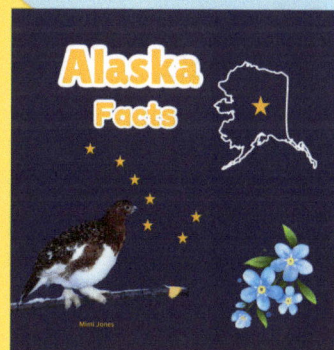

Alaska Facts

www.mimibooks.com

www.ingramcontent.com/pod-product-compliance
Lightning Source LLC
Chambersburg PA
CBHW041549040426
42447CB00002B/109